HOW TO BUILD TRUST IN A RELATIONSHIP

Powerful Ways to Rebuild Effective Communication, Resolve Conflict, Improve Intimacy, And Avoid Betrayal

By

CLAIRE ROBIN

Other Books by the Same Author

I want to thank you for purchasing this book. I hope that after reading this book you will achieve the wisdom to improve your relationship effectively. Below are other books on building a successful relationship and marriage. This is for you who want to cultivate a better relationship:

1. <u>200 Ways to Seduce Your Husband:</u> How to Boost Your Marriage Libido and Actually Enjoy Sex: A Couple's Intimacy Guide

2. <u>232 Questions for Couples</u>: Romantic Relationship Conversation Starters for Connecting, Building Trust, and Emotional Intimacy

3. <u>Communication in Marriage:</u> How to Communicate Effectively With Your Spouse, Build Trust and Rekindle Love

4. Anger Management in Marriage: Ways to Control Your Emotions, Get Healed of Hurts & Respond to Offenses (Overcome Bad Temper)

5. 100 Ways to Cultivate Intimacy in Your Marriage: How to Improve Communication, Build Trust and Rekindle Love

6. 40 Bible Verses to Pray Over Your Husband and Marriage: Powerful Scriptural Prayers for Protection, Guidance, Wisdom, Companionship, Commitment, Healing, and Deliverance

7. Sexual Intimacy in Marriage: 100 Facts Nobody Ever Told You About Sex and Romance

"A relationship without trust is like a car without gas, you can stay in it all you want, but it won't go anywhere."

"Maybe your relationship is different, maybe no one has written a novel about the kind of growth you will encounter in your relationship yet. Maybe you are required to write the novel with every day that you live, improving with time and allowing love and trust to become your ultimate motivation."

"In building a strong relationship, doing nothing is as good as doing something. Sometimes you do better by not doing anything at all"

"There comes a point in a relationship when you realize you trust someone enough to let them keep their secrets."

Table of Contents

Introduction 9

Discover 13

Earn The Trust 18

Keeping Secrets 24

The Judging Partner 31

Forgiving Over and Over Again 34

Working On Your Personal Growths ... 38

Disagreeing The Right Way 45

Other Books by the Same Author 50

Introduction

Trust is apparently the backbone of every reasonable relationship. For a relationship to last and be beneficial, two people most come together and have a reasonable level of trust on the intentions, decisions and the activities of one another.

Trust cannot be decided or pronounced, trust is built from one level to the other. Just the way you need a proof in order to trust someone with your interest, extreme love and commitment, the other person also needs the same capacity of proof in order to trust you.

Words alone cannot earn trust, only the deceitful find refuge under the wings or word play. Trust and lack of it are very important in detecting a healthy relationship.

People only trust you automatically when they want you to trust their deceits. People find it hard to trust people who completely look trustworthy, especially in a committed relationship.

Only when someone care about your trust will they work hard in making sure that they trust you. Only if someone loves you that much, will they want to trust the safety of every decision and action you take.

Building trust in a relationship might take some time but once built, comfort and happiness will be experienced.

You will be able to reach a level of deeper intimacy where you can actually share everything with your partner, with the hope that they are doing the same.

Also, you will trust that your business is not shared with strangers in the outside world. Intimacy will be built and you will experience less challenges when it comes to communicating effectively in your relationship.

Keep in mind that trust is not the matter of decision. Trust is something you build, and you have to allow your partner to take the step in earning your trust even as you work your part to make sure that trust is becomes permanent in your relationship.

Discover

Try to find out what trust means to your partner. Different people interpret trust differently.

Part of getting to know your partner very well is determining the kind of thing he or she measures as trust.

Also, you need to have a proper self-actualization in order to determine exactly what trust means to you as a person.

Write down your concerns, what would hurt you the most, and the things that could be done outside trust.

One way to understand this is by openly communicating your expectations with your partner.

Let your needs be put on the table, choose the ones you can meet now and the ones you have to put a long lasting effort to achieve.

Many couples in the normal world tend to shy away from these kind of conversations.

In fact, couples should be able to sit down in serenity and work on their communication skills. Being scared of pushing someone away is one of the red flags of unhealthy relationships.

You need to be able to talk about anything, and be careful about nothing. The flexibility of communication is the only way to discover your partner really well.

Your needs should be expressed regularly. You should be able to communicate in order to get rid of assumptions and misconceptions about your partner and relationship as a whole.

Disagreements will occur and that will give you the chance to understand each other even better.

Betrayal may come on your way in building great relationship, but that will help you understand the weaknesses you have and what step to take in order to provide the right support system for your partner so that they will be stronger next time they are met with a similar challenge.

You need to take the time to understand your partner beyond what they are saying.

You need to watch their reactions, defensiveness and vulnerability.

Do not criticize their weakness so they won't be afraid to voice out their needs.

Only when the other person is comfortable with sharing sensitive issues will they actually maintain a good communication, thus greater level of trust.

Discovery is the perfect place to start when it comes to building and maintaining trust.

Earn The Trust

As said before, building trust takes a gradual process. The process of earning trust takes even longer. You need to give it time. But constant effort always makes the difference.

You need to stop taking trust for granted and start treating it as priority in your relationship.

Try as much as possible to stick to your words and always be clear about your intentions. Your actions should define your words and you should not deviate for any reason.

Make sure you have a reasonable reason to deviate from your words, and even if you have to, make sure you make contact with your partner before you change anything.

Let the perceptions of your personality be certain. You cannot earn your partner's trust if they cannot actually rely on you as a person.

You need to be stable with your actions and decisions. Meaning, you need to stick to one thing and only change when necessary.

You need to be stable and consistent in all your dealings so that winning will become the language.

KEEPING YOUR PROMISES

Failing to keep your promises over and over again will never do any good to your effort in building trust in your relationship.

Focus actually on keeping the promises regardless how much it will cost you. In relationship, you have to realize that your happiness matters as much as the happiness of the other person. Sometimes you will need to deprive yourself the comfort in order to make sure the other person is happy, and most importantly, to keep your promises.

Do not overlook the little things you do every day. Those things really matter in building up your partner's perception towards the relationship and you as a person.

Treat the small things as much as you will treat the big ones. Simply calling your partner when you are late will make the difference.

Remembering to take the item from the grocery store as promised, paying the bills on time, etc., can go a long way especially if you are heading for a long term relationship.

Keeping Secrets

In relationship, most partners don't know the difference between keeping secrets **for** each other and keeping secrets **from** each other.

Keeping secrets for each other:

Keeping your personal conversations in the confinement of your home.

Not letting your friends or other family members to interfere with the affairs of your relationship.

Discussing every plan with your partner about the people outside, and not saying a word to the people outside about mentioning it to your partner.

Taking the steps towards something new in your relationship, and not sharing it with people until it manifests.

Keeping the financial details, challenges, and struggles to yourselves in the home, and not sharing with strangers, unless they are professional financial advisors.

Keeping secretes from each other:

Getting a raise and never sharing the details with your partner.

Passing through a financial challenge and making sure that your partner is left in the dark even when you have contacted several friends.

Actually, allowing your partner to find out about something that involves you outside instead of you.

Only talking about something when your partner brings it up in a conversation.

With these examples you can be able to categorize and realize when you are keeping secrets for your partner or from them.

Although some details have to be kept a secret to protect their feelings, you need to make sure that you remain open in all your endeavors.

COMMUNICATING OPENLY AND IN PERSON

Do not communicate the most sensitive part of your relationship in public. Take your time to talk about important matters when everyone is in a good mood and you can talk for a considerable time.

Important subject matters should be treated with care and you don't need to rush your conversations. You don't want to lose the true meaning or reason for your conversation just because you have a lot of things to discuss.

When having a conversation, do not drift to something else. Focus on one single thing and make sure that you reach a better understanding.

Also, do not text important details especially when it is sensitive and can raise questions on the side of your partner.

Only bring something up when you are with that person in the physical. Making sure you are clear and reconfirming the message your partner is trying to send is very important so that you won't take misconceptions to bed. Do not allow miscommunication to ruin your intimacy.

The Judging Partner

Your partner does not supposed to be understandable all the time at each and every level of your intimacy.

It is your responsibility to try as much as possible to try to understand your partner even when they are confused. You need to understand why something becomes so important to your partner.

Also, communicating well with your spouse will help you achieve this level of understanding.

Do not weight the importance of an issue based on your feelings or knowledge, weight it based on the fact that your partner sees it as important. This way you won't feel the need or impulse to judge the decisions of your partner.

Thus trust can be built, and respect will be cultivated due time. In the process of building trust, respect is very important.

Your partner needs to be assured that you trust and respect the things they treasure and you have to make sure that your partner would trust your devotion and the things you treasure apart from them.

Forgiving Over and Over Again

Mistakes happen, and some mistakes might even cost the trust you have for someone. In the realistic world, you are required to forgive as much as you can handle.

Forgiving might not always mean forgetting, but you should try as much as possible not to allow the mistakes of your partner to influence the level of your diligent, passion, commitment and even trust.

Instead of finding ways to criticize their mistakes, make a plan to support them so they won't repeat that same mistake.

Also, be the one to constantly remind and caution them whenever they are about to be exposed to a situation that make them vulnerable.

Do not hold on to pass transgressions just the way you won't like your spouse or partner to hold on to the past.

Make a decision to get rid of the resentment or the feeling of lost when your partner repeats the same mistake over and over again. Feel the ability to make mistakes. Never to be perfect but to build each other, to grow in love, reaching to the perfect level of a committed relationship.

Accept the apology over and over again and let go of the hurt continuously.

Do not allow yourself to become unhappy just because your partner is not following the conventional script for building a better relationship.

Maybe your relationship is different, maybe no one has written a novel about the kind of growth you will encounter in your relationship yet. Maybe you are required to write the novel with every day that you live, improving with time and allowing love and trust to become your ultimate motivation.

Working On Your Personal Growths

Personal growth is one of the most important requirements for building a healthy relationship. Starting from self-esteem to self-actualization, proper self-growth is very important so that you will have a definitive requirement for the other person in your relationship.

Once you are able to define your level and the kind of treatment you want to receive, you will attract characteristics that will bring about respect for those criteria you set for yourself.

You don't need a new person to be able to cultivate such energy. All you need is some amount of self-love, which would entail taking care of yourself intensely, knowing what you want emotionally, avoiding the wrong people, relating at a proper level with different people, improving your knowledge or skills professionally, reading relationship books and the books that will bring about awareness about human behavior.

Going through all these, you will discover a new dimension. You will begin to feel differently about yourself and how you want people to treat you. Then you will begin to require them to treat you that way.

Having high level of understanding of how people and the environment affect you, there will be change in the way you handle relationship.

You will become more truthful and you will cultivate respect, which ultimately means your partner will respect you as much, not to lie to you or go behind your back. Thus the end result will ultimately become trust.

BEING SUPPORTIVE

Make your partner realize the fact that you are trying to build trust in your relationship. Give them support and also expect to get a full support.

Not only in building trust, you need to be extremely supportive of each other's interests. There is always an insecurity and mistrust about your intentions whenever you begin to disagree with your partner's effort towards something.

So, your lack of support may slow down the level of growth you suppose to achieve even as you take your relationship to the next level.

The support also counts when you are trying new things. Encourage your partner to take the risk inasmuch as there is a tendency for elevation.

Let them become comfortable with mistakes just because you are around. The devastating part is when you allow them to get comfortable with taking risks without your support.

Do not allow them to realize how well they can do without you, so that your attention and commitment will be needed all the time. Simply, allow them to live their truths even as you allow yourself to be their support system.

Disagreeing The Right Way

Do not allow the outside world to see you arguing or generally disagreeing about something personal.

Your partner may say something while discussing in the public forum that might not sit with you, wait until you get back home and you can settle that.

Going against your partner openly might humiliate them or even backfire to humiliate you.

Also, this behavior will generally affect the level of trust you have when it comes to calling each other out in the public.

Your partner may begin to doubt if you are keeping your relationship business at the confinement of your home, and the amount of control you have when you are upset even in the public.

These will affect also the level of effort they are putting in making sure that your lines of communications are intact.

Also, waiting until you are alone with your partner will give you time to construct a better way of approaching your spouse to get them to talk really deep with you. Respect will be built and honesty will be encouraged all in all.

What's Next?

Building trust is the hardest part of committed relationship, but once built you will enjoy every bit of time you spend with this one person you treasure. Respect and understanding becomes the backbone of trust and harmony.

All your effort could be useless if you fail to respect your words. Simply, **do what you promised to do.**

When frustration begins to build because of failure on the side of your partner, do the right thing and just sit back. Sometimes doing nothing is as important as doing something.

Other Books by the Same Author

1. 200 Ways to Seduce Your Husband: How to Boost Your Marriage Libido and Actually Enjoy Sex: A Couple's Intimacy Guide

2. 232 Questions for Couples: Romantic Relationship Conversation Starters for Connecting, Building Trust, and Emotional Intimacy

3. Communication in Marriage: How to Communicate Effectively With Your Spouse, Build Trust and Rekindle Love

4. Anger Management in Marriage: Ways to Control Your Emotions, Get Healed of Hurts & Respond to Offenses (Overcome Bad Temper)

5. 100 Ways to Cultivate Intimacy in Your Marriage: How to Improve Communication, Build Trust and Rekindle Love

6. <u>40 Bible Verses to Pray Over Your Husband and Marriage:</u> Powerful Scriptural Prayers for Protection, Guidance, Wisdom, Companionship, Commitment, Healing, and Deliverance

7. <u>Sexual Intimacy in Marriage:</u> 100 Facts Nobody Ever Told You About Sex and Romance

Made in the USA
Lexington, KY
12 February 2019